Passive Income Ideas

Passive Income Streams to Make You $1,000 to $10,000 Per Month and Help You Achieve Financial Freedom (Stock Market, Affiliate Marketing, Real Estate, Options Trading and More!)

Richard James

Table Of Contents

Introduction

First of all, I would like to thank you for downloading *Passive Income Ideas: Passive Income Streams To Make You $1,000 to $10,000 Per Month and Help You Achieve Financial Freedom (Stock Market, Affiliate Marketing, Real Estate, Options Trading and More!)*. This book was created for people looking to diversify their income streams and to start earning money on the side or to start making full-time income solely from these income streams. In the present day and age, people still tend to believe in having one full-time job for 30 to 40 years and having fun after they retire while saving as much as they can before retirement hits them. Hence, if that's what you want to do, then great! If not, then you don't need to be stuck with one stream of income for the rest of your life.

There are people right now making money while sitting at home or on a vacation—making money online or anywhere else and letting it be passive is quite possible in this day and age. We are truly blessed to be living in this era where we have the opportunity to make money passively—so don't wait for the life you want to live in 30 to 40 years. Live it now! You can truly do it with the help of this book.

In the following chapters, we will be going through things that will help you make passive income online or offline as well as provide you with the tools you will need to do so. More specifically, in Chapter One, we will talk about what exactly passive income is and what kind of mentality it takes to get it. In the second chapter, we will talk about Affiliate Marketing, one of the many ways to make passive income. Therefore, to cut to the case, we will show you the top ways to make passive income today.

Trust me, guys and girls—once you get a hang of these passive income streams and once you put in some of your time and effort into them, you will start to create something truly beautiful and amazing. There is no better feeling than knowing that you have enough money to do whatever you want in life. We were meant to live a happy, free life—so let's make it so!

Why Should You Have a Passive Income Stream?

Now, before you start this book, I want to make one thing very clear—this book does not guarantee that you will make money with these income streams. Some readers might make a lot of money from this, and some won't make a single dime. Just make sure you are aware of this before you take any actions on the information provided in this book, as the author will not accept any responsibility for your losses.

People don't realize how important it is to have multiple streams of income in this day and age. Nowadays, everything is a lot more expensive— from rent, food, cars, and even gas. Unfortunately, average salaries are just not going to cut it. Hence, for us to live a life free of financial stress, we need to create our own streams of income on the side. Now, this sounds great and all, but how would you start earning extra cash? Is it by taking up a part-time job? No, you do it by making money passively.

To make sure everyone knows what I am talking about, let me define what *passive income* really is. Passive income is a type of income that is reacquired on a monthly or weekly basis and takes little to no effort.

Having said that, let's talk about what it takes to start your very own passive income streams.

Truth be told—it takes some work to start earning money passively. There isn't a way you can punch in a couple of numbers and start making an extra $1,000 to $10,000 a month—it could take a couple of months or even years before it indeed becomes passive. However, once it *finally* does, you will not regret the hard work you put in to start earning some serious cash while sitting at home watching TV.

The best part about these income streams, which I will be sharing with you in this book, is that there is no limit to the amount of income you can generate. The more time, effort, and money you put into it—the more money you can make. What I am trying to say is this: if your life goal is to become a millionaire, you can do it with this income stream—however, for you to be able to do that, you will have to work hard on it and have the right mindset.

Let's discuss the world's top earners and what their mentality is like. Jeff Bezos started his company Amazon in the early 90s with a goal in mind. His goal, in the beginning, was to sell books, as he stated in one of his interviews that "Books have the greatest number of categories compared to any other products out there—and to sell them on the internet, which is still growing, would be a great idea." He knew what others couldn't think about. He was thinking in the future, which is why he is now worth $150 billion.

Mark Zuckerberg created Facebook because he wanted people to connect more efficiently. This led to the creation of Facebook, one of the best ways to communicate with your friends and family. What Mark Zuckerberg did was thinking in the future. He remembered what he can do to make human communication better for now and for the years to come.

Here is what I am trying to convey—for you to be successful like Mark Zuckerberg and Jeff Bezos, you need to think outside the box. You really need to start thinking like you are going to change the world with your business or whatever you decide to do. One more thing to remember is this: never give up.

Do you think that building Amazon from the ground up was a smooth-sailing task? Do you think that getting Facebook to where it as at now was an easy job? Probably not. So, if you are looking to become successful, you need to remember that there will always be adversities coming your way and that you might experience some failures in the process. Just remember that these failures are a part of the journey—so don't give up, keep pushing through, and learn from your mistakes so that eventually, just like Jeff Bezos and Mark Zuckerberg, you *will* make it.

The information provided in this book can make you extra cash on the side or can even make you a millionaire. Regardless of your goal, you will need to put in some effort—and most of the time, how much effort you put into a specific task will yield more results.

Just know that all these income streams I will be sharing with you can genuinely be passive, but the only catch is that you will need to do some work before it starts to become passive— and for all the guys or girls trying to become a millionaire with these income streams that will be shared in this book, just be aware of the hard work you might have to do and the tough times you might have to face. But remember— there is light outside of the tunnel, and just like Mark Zuckerberg and Jeff Bezos, if you push through the hard work and tough times, you *can* and you *will* make it!

Affiliate Marketing

The first income stream we will be covering is Affiliate Marketing. The best way to describe Affiliate Marketing would be to use an analogy. Let us say you are the president of your university, and every single student in that university listens to your voice. Since you are the president of this university, a majority of the people in that university follows your advice and recommendations—when suddenly, a professor of the university offers you to sell his textbook, and in return, you get a commission or a percentage of the textbook sale by promoting the professor's textbook to your audience or following.

Thus, in essence, this would be an example of Affiliate Marketing. Simply what you have to do in order to get sales would be first to create a big following and then promote a product to that audience. Simple enough, right? Well, there are some tricks involved in this method in order to become successful in Affiliate Marketing, which we will be discussing further in this chapter. Now, there are a lot of ways you can start to market a product to make a commission—we will be discussing how to do so by using the best methods for you to start Affiliate Marketing.

Now, the methods that will help you start making money with Affiliate Marketing will be

YouTube, blogging, Instagram/Facebook page. Now, these three are the best ways to get started with your Affiliate Marketing business. There are some pros and cons to each of these tools—you might have to try out all three methods before you can see which one works for you and which one doesn't. Without further ado, let's begin with YouTube.

YouTube

YouTube was founded on February 14th, 2005, created by three former PayPal employees Chad Hurley, Steve Chen, and Jawed Karim. YouTube at first was created by the founders to share videos easily without facing any problems while doing so, Fast forward to November 2006 when YouTube was sold to Google for USD 1.65. Ever since then YouTube has not stopped growing, according to some sources there is at least 1 billion hours' worth of videos are being watched every day on YouTube. That goes to show how big YouTube is, now you might be wondering since this website is so popular you could easily start promoting affiliate products and earn some great commissions.

Well, there are some tricks involved to do so, although there are a lot of videos watched on YouTube on any given the time of day there is still some things you need to make sure is in check from your end before you can really start to promote your product on this website. Don't worry it isn't hard, just like any business it will take some time and effort to get started.

The first thing you will need to is to create a niche. Really think about what are you interested in. For example, if you are interested in fitness, then make a fitness channel. If you are interested in science, make a Science channel. The main thing you need to consider before you start your very own YouTube channel is to make sure that whatever your channel is about, it needs to be something you are genuinely interested in. This is the reason why people can see through everything these days. If you hate fitness and you decide to make a fitness channel, they can tell that you don't like fitness-related stuff, and therefore they won't subscribe to your channel. Making sure you have love and passion for the circuit you will be building on YouTube is imperative.

The second thing we need to worry about is growing your channel or following, and if you don't have an audience on your YouTube channel, then chances are your Affiliate Marketing endeavors might go to fail. So, you first need to grow your YouTube channel before you can start selling affiliate products. With that being said, let us discuss how you can build your YouTube channel fast and efficiently.

Now there are a lot of ways to do so, but the best way I would recommend is to come up with unique content. I know it sounds super cliché, but it works! Think about it why would someone want to follow you if you don't have something different to offer them. So, there are a lot of ways to be incompatible with your content, but the primary technique to make different material is to think outside the box and into the future like what would be the "new thing." Once you have figured it out, make sure you are the first one to start the trend.

Another way to start getting some more views and followers would be to have an exciting caption and clickbait. Let me give you an example of click bait. Recently, big YouTubers would do things like "My yearly income" and a photo of them with money as the clickbait on the video. Since everyone is curious about how much these big YouTubers make, these YouTubers directly allude people into their video and start to rank up the views, but they never reveal their income. As I said, it is merely clickbait. Now, this technique does work, but you can't use it every time as it will lead to some drops in your followers etc. so use it with caution.

Finally, the last technique I would recommend would be to collaborate with YouTubers who already have a big following. Before you work with one of the big YouTube channels, make sure their channel is related to your channel. Collaborating with a bigger channel won't be easy or free. I would say 1 out of 10 will agree upon doing a "collab video" with you and finally work out a deal either by an upfront payment or a shared partnership of the video. There is some money involved, but it is totally worth it as this technique works the best in order to grow your YouTube channel and business.

Now, after you have managed to grow your YouTube channel to a substantial level—ideally a 100k followers or subscribers—it would take no time to promote products from which you can earn an affiliate commission. Again, remember to promote a product which is related specifically to your YouTube channel. Don't expect to sell a PlayStation 4 on a channel related to fitness. It is not that people won't buy—they probably won't—but it makes you look like a salesman, which is not the look that you should be going for. So, if you want to earn some affiliate commission, make sure the product is related to your channel and niche.

There are many websites you can use to start earning an affiliate commission, but the two leading websites I would recommend is ClickBank and Amazon. Let us cover ClickBank first. ClickBank is an online video course website that sells courses from a health-related niche to a making-money-online niche, so as you can see, it has a broad spectrum of courses available on its website. You can earn up to 75% of the commissions on each sale, and it is straightforward to do so if you have a following. All you have to do is review the video course and give your audience an honest review of the product. Make sure you add your affiliate link in the description below of the YouTube channel in order to earn commissions.

The second one is Amazon. As we know, Amazon is the biggest e-commerce website in the world right now. On top of that, they sell anything you can imagine, so it doesn't matter what niche you are in; you can find a related product to your niche. That said, there are some pros and cons to this website. The cons are that the commission rates are lower compared to ClickBank. There is no exact percentage of commission you will get, but 75% of commission on Amazon is super hard to find as compared to ClickBank. Now the positive is that once someone even clicks your affiliate link, you will be getting a commission on everything they buy for the next 48 hours. This is where the lower commission rate makes up for Amazon. Again, if you decide to use Amazon as your source of affiliate partner, make sure you try out the product and give a proper review.

Blogging

Let us talk about blogging and using it to market products and earn Affiliate Marketing commissions. Just like YouTube, blogging is a great way to make Affiliate Marketing commissions. You can say blogging is the godfather of Affiliate Marketing, as that's what started this whole "Affiliate Marketing" trend. Just like YouTube, you need to get steady traffic to your blog before you can begin to make some money from it.

Now, there are a lot of ways to drive traffic to your blog, and they are quite similar to YouTube's way of attracting traffic, but we will only discuss the main three methods you can use to start advertising your blogs right now.

The first method is getting free traffic from other blogs and forums. Let's say your blog is related to fitness. What you will do is find a popular blog and its discussions online. If it is a forum, then it's recommended that you truly become a part of the forum and start asking questions and answering questions. Once you truly begin to feel like you are becoming a part of the conference, then slowly begin to link your blogs into the forum post which will help you get more traffic to your blog. You see, doing this will help you get more traffic to your blog where you will start to promote your products. Now if it is a blog, then I would just recommend you put a link to your blog in the comment sections of the larger, more famous blog. This will also help you get traffic.

The second method to get some traffic to your blog would be to become a guest writer on a more popular blog. This might require you to invest some money, but it is totally worth it. Basically, what you will do is to first contact a blog related to your niche, which is already getting a lot of traffic. Second, you will have to either pay the blog owner to feature you in his or blog or if he/she is gracious enough, he/she would feature you in the blog for free. Make sure to leave a link to your blog on their website, so the people following his or her blog can start following you.

Collecting emails—now this method works the best! In order for you to make some affiliate sales, you will need to make sure people see your affiliate products. Making sure you collect emails of every person that visits your blog will boost your sales, how you do that is simple. Offer something for free, so if your blog is about fitness, offer them a free workout plan in lure of their email. Now, here is what you will be doing with this email list. I want you to only start sending out emails to your list whenever you upload a blog, make sure you don't spam them every day. Email them once a week, ideally. Emailing people will ensure you get as many visitors to your blog as possible, which would mean more chances of you closing a sale.

Instagram/Facebook Page

This is also an amazing technique to start earning those affiliate commissions. So how this works is quite similar to YouTube. You will first need to attract a following to your page, then you can start to promote your products slowly. Now to explain this process rather simply is this: no following = no sales.

Therefore, our main goal is to start getting our Instagram page bigger, which would equate to more affiliate commission.

The first method would be setting up a Facebook page which would be specific to your niche. Now after you have created an Instagram account and a Facebook page, start promoting both pages only by purchasing shout-outs from bigger pages related to your niche. After that is done, you will slowly begin to grow your Instagram/Facebook page, but one thing to remember is that you don't want to stop posting content on your Instagram/Facebook page as it will result to a drop of followers and engagement rate.

The second method to grow your Instagram page is to use a technique known as "follow-unfollow." It is pretty self-explanatory. What you have to do is follow users hoping that they would follow you back and then eventually unfollow them. This technique works if your goal is to gain some following quickly. That said, this is not the best way for long-term growth so keep that in mind. Start following people and unfollow them after three days or so.

Finally, let us talk about how to make money with Affiliate Marketing on Instagram. So, after you have a following off around 100k, you will then start to notice people will pay you money to have their product on your page. You can also do Affiliate Marketing with ClickBank, but it just works better when you promote on Instagram using the "shout-out" technique.

Using All Three at Once

Now, ideally, this is how it should be. Using YouTube, Blogging, and Instagram all at once will yield you the best results. So, if you really want to make some serious cash with Affiliate Marketing, here is how you do it. You will first create a brand. For example, if you're into fitness, you will create a YouTube channel, blog, and Instagram/Facebook account with a brand name that you came up with. Now you will merely use all the techniques listed in this chapter to make sure all three sales channels— YouTube, blog, and Instagram—grow and flourish.

How Much Money Can You Make?

Now, this is a question that can't be answered straight away. You see, if your goal is to put in minimal time and make it as passive as possible, you can realistically make anywhere from $100 to $1,000 a month. But if you really want to make some serious cash and if you utilize all three sales channels while using the techniques above, you can make $100,000 to $1,000,000 a month. I have personally seen some pay stubs of the top Affiliate Marketers, and they surely make more than a million dollars a year, so if you are willing to put in the hard work, you can seriously make some fantastic cash.

All that said, I would now like to conclude this chapter by saying this: With Affiliate Marketing, the choice is yours. You can choose to make an extra $1,000 a month by doing some work here and there or you can honestly take your income to the next level! Again, the choice is yours

Stock Market

The stock market is also a form of trading. It has been used by big investors like Warren Buffet to make some serious cash. The stock market was founded on March 8th, 1817 in New York City, U.S.A. The stock market was created for people to start investing in companies for the company to get more funds for growth. Eventually, as the companies would grow, the stock prices would go up for the specific company. Thus, the people who had some money invested in the company would sell those stocks for a profit, which would mean more money in their pockets. So, in a nutshell, that is how stock market trading was invented.

Now, this method has some pros and cons to it, so let us go through them. To start with the advantages, the first positive is, of course, you can make money using this process, the second positive would be it is entirely passive compared to other methods in this book all you have to do is checkup the stock market frequently, and you should be good. Just like anything in this world, there are some cons. The first significant con would be that you can lose you invested money. It is imperative that you do your research on the company before you decide to invest in that company.

The second con would be irregular—let's say you buy a stock at $1.30 apiece and a couple of days go by and the stock is now $2.00 apart most of the people would rather wait, but sometimes the stock would come plummeting down to $0.80 a piece which would make you lose money. Or if you decide to sell it at $2.00 per share, you would still make good money but if the next day it shot up to $3.00 per share you would be regretting your decision.

Look, what I am trying to say is this. Utilizing the stock market to make money is like a rollercoaster ride, you will have your ups and downs, and you will face some significant losses sometimes or some significant gains. Although there are ways to avoid the significant injuries with the methods I will provide, the main thing to remember is not to get greedy as it might make money sometimes, but you can come crashing down.

There are two methods to make money utilizing the stock market which we will be going through today, the first one is "Growth stocks" and the second one would be "Mutual funds."

Growth Stocks

Growth stocks, also known as "buy low sell high" is one the most common techniques used by many investors, although this method takes time and effort it can yield you with some good returns. Now the principle behind this method is this, find a company with cost per stock is low and then once it goes up sell it and enjoy the profits you made. Simple enough right? Well, there are some things to be learned before you go about doing so, specifically three things.

1. Researching About the Company
2. Patients and Discipline
3. Continued Research

To begin with, let's talk about how to research the company you will be investing in. As we know, there are a lot of companies in this day and age, picking out the right company to spend it can be rather difficult. So, this is where the extensive research comes in before you pay in one. To be clear, there is no right or wrong company to be investing in. There are a lot of companies which will go up, and you have to pick one you believe in. To find out if the stocks of a certain company will go up or not it requires a couple of steps, the first thing you need to do is to check out last year's report on the company and their stock prices.

Check to see if the stock prices have steadily been going up or not and is it still continuing on, the second method would be to make sure that the company is up to do something big which will help the company grow, for example, Canada made marijuana legal which equated to all the marijuana dispensaries stock prices to go up in Canada. So, what I mean by doing research, is to see if anything significant is happening to the company or the market the company is in.

Being patient and having a certain amount of discipline is imperative for your growth and success in this market in order for you to make money and not to lose money while investing in stocks, Truth be told you can make some severe cash overnight with this method or make some fantastic returns a couple of years down the road. Don't get impatient and sell your stocks when you have an idea of the company and if it is going to be making significant moves soon.

On the other hand, don't get greedy. If the stocks are coming up fast, then they will come down just as soon in most cases. Don't get greedy wanting for more money sell it once you have made some good money out of those stocks. This would be where your discipline comes into factor. Finally, I would like to you remember that investing in stocks requires some "gut feeling," not everything is going to be calculated in stock market spending. After you have done your research and decided to buy stocks, you might have to go by gut feelings sometimes to sell your shares.

Finally, what you will have to take care of is continued research on the company, now making sure stay up to date with the company's news in which you invested in is imperative for your growth and success. This will give you an idea of when to sell and when not to sell your stock, for instance, let us say you find out the company you invested in might notice a drop in its stock price. Merely make sure to sell it before you lose money or visa-versa, continued research and updates will give you an idea of when to sell and when not to sell.

Mutual Funds

This method is a little bit easier to get started with as it comes with lower risk, mutual funds are when your money is managed by professionals and is invested in different companies by them. Although there is a cut taken by the professionals, in the end, it still is still a safer and effective way if you want to make money as compared to "Growth Stock." Since you won't have to worry about doing research online and checking out every little detail about the company, it will be more of a "passive investment" which will make you money later on.

So, if you want to make money without spending too much time doing research and other things which are related to "growth stocks" as it is less of a risk, go ahead, but you won't make as much money as you could be making with "growth stocks."

How Much Money Can You Make?

Now, this would depend entirely on the market and how much you put in, the stocks game "is the more you put in, the more money you will make" so if you want to make more you will have to invest more. So, there is no estimate on how much you can potentially make, you can make $1,000 profit up to a $1,000,000 profit it depends on luck and how much you invest in the company. Like I said previously if you want to play it safe, I would recommend you invest in some mutual funds, even though the returns won't be as good as "growth stocks" it will still yield you some good money without the risk.

With that note, I would like to conclude this chapter today. Remember that investing in the stock market is a gamble, you might make some money or lose some money. If you do what is advised in this book chances are you will make money, many full-time day traders make money solely off the stock market. But you need to remember that the market is unpredictable and anything could happen anytime, so if I where you I would invest some money on the side rather than to make this a full-time job as it is not so secure. Once you do spend, don't forget to do your research and to make sure that you don't pay more than what you can afford. Again if "growth stocks" scare you then invest in some mutual funds. Sometimes it is good to take some risks as you don't know where it will take you, remember to be safe and smart with your money and don't get too greedy as it could lead you to lose your hard-earned money which is the last thing we want to do.

Real Estate

Investing in real estate is one of the best ways to make passive income, but it does require you to make some upfront investment. Now, please be aware that this chapter will be a lot more "theoretical" and with a lot more bullet points as compared to others—so read it a couple of times to really get its essence.

Investing in real estate has some great benefits! You can really make some excellent side income out of it.

How Does Real Estate Investment Work?

To make money in real estate, one thing you have to remember is to have a positive cash flow, meaning at the end of the month you should have made more money compared to what you spent on it.

The question is: Should you sell or rent out? Rent it out. As long as you hold on to the property, the value will go up, so it is always recommended to rent it out rather than selling it.

In order to make money off real estate you will have to buy a property, and regardless of what property it is, you will have to invest a lump-sum of cash. For most of the people, this would mean getting a mortgage. This would equate to a long-term commitment. Once you decide to rent out your property, you will have to use the income generated by the rent to cover all your in-house expenses like repairs etc. So, if you have the funds, buy cash so you can start making some serious profits from the beginning rather than waiting 15 to 20 years.

Investing in Real Estate

I can understand how everyone won't have the lump-sum money to spend on a property. There are a few ways to secure a property rental if you look hard enough:

- Sell assets you do have like your car, jewelry or stocks and bonds.

- Find an investment partner.

- Get a loan privately.

- Take out a mortgage.

- Take over the mortgage payments of someone who is in financial distress and cannot afford it themselves.

The Financial Costs

If you can't find the full amount, then it is highly recommended that you pay as much as you can as a down payment. This can lower the monthly repayments you will be responsible for. Also, on taking a mortgage, you should be prepared to cover the costs for a few months while waiting for a tenant.

Now, the rent you will be asking for your new property will depend on a lot of factors. Depending on the size of the house and neighborhood, it can vary.

Deciding the rate of your renting.

The rent you ask for is the most critical determinant in your real estate investment endeavors. So how do you go about setting a rent rate that will provide you with the best returns and be attractive to potential tenants?

The first thing to do is to find reasonably-priced real estate you can afford. It is also advised, to keep in mind that you should not invest in a rental property if the purchase price is twelve times more than what you expect to receive in rent for a year.

Factors to Consider When Calculating Rent

First of all, do some research and find out the average rent in your area. Deduct related essential expenses such as mortgage repayments, real estate taxes and insurance costs (remember to divide each of these cost factors by 12) and maintenance and repairs fees (set aside a healthy allowance for these costs).

In the beginning, asking for too high of a rent rate may lead you not to find a suitable tenant easily, and your rental sits empty for a few months. At the same time, you need to make sure you don't underestimate what maintenance will cost you, and you end up paying more than you budgeted for.

Your maintenance and repairs costs will depend on how old your property is, who your tenants are and how well they look after it so, for example, a house with young students may require more regarding cosmetic repair than a home with more mature tenants. The third consideration is whether maintenance will be D-I-Y or outsourced to a contractor or handled via a real estate management agency for a monthly management fee.

D-I-Y repairs mean lowered costs but the inconvenience of being available 24/7 should an emergency arise.

Finding the right balance between a fair market-related rate and a good value tenant and you have found the perfect formula for consistent and favorable returns on your real estate rental investment for the long term.

Do Your Research.

You will need to conduct a thorough real estate search before you purchase your first buy-to-let property. In your search, you will need to base your choice on a number of factors. A good piece of advice is to look very carefully at the location, even if the property seems a bit run down but the area is excellent, it promises greater returns over the long term, and if you have some more money to invest in the future fix it up it will only lead you to make more money.

Slowly Build Up.

Managing more than one piece of property can be overwhelming for anyone regardless it is an experienced landlord or not. Starting off with rental real estate requires a learning curve, slowly invest and it shall grow. If you want to, you can start by renting out your basement or room. Slowly build up from there.

Property Types to Invest In

As you become a real estate investor, there are choices of property types to choose from. All of them have advantages and disadvantages to each, so picking them based on your need is imperative.

There are some types of real estate that are more ideal for beginner property investors to get their feet wet, so to speak. Here are a few suggestions on what kind of property that offers favorable advantages.

Single-Family Homes

This is the most comfortable property to find tenants for. Many new families or couples choose single-family homes as their preferred choice for long-term rentals. This type of real estate investment makes it an ideal opportunity for a beginner investor as they offer better tenant quality value, which means more financially stable, more likely to look after the property and pay rent regularly. The single-family home is a detached or a semi-detached property unit with a yard or driveway as a distinct dividing line from neighboring properties.

Advantages:

- Investing in the property can greatly increase the price you bought it for.

- Provides greater returns on investment over the long-term.

- Provided it is located in a growing neighborhood with great family people, and it was well maintained the property would grow its resale value.

- Property taxes will be lower as compared to multi-family units and commercial real estate.

- Management costs are lower if your tenants are great tenants.

Disadvantages:

- Cash flow is dependent on one, unlike multi-family units. If a tenant moves out and you have to wait a while for another, the empty house could cause you to pay for the mortgage for the times it is left without a tenant.

Multi-Family House

This type of real estate can be comprised of duplexes, triplexes, or quadplexes on a single plot. A housing can be accommodated for two to four families. Each unit provides a rental opportunity. This type of real estate is easier to maintain and manage as compared to having more than one single family units to look after.

Advantages:

- More financing options available for the investor.

- If one tenant leaves, cash flow is still generated from the tenants of the other units.

- If you, the owner, lives in one of the units, you can benefit from the owner-occupied mortgage rate.

Disadvantages:

- The tenant pool for multi-family rentals is smaller, so there are few buyers when you do decide to resell.

- Buying multi-family units are relatively more expensive than single family homes.

- Repairs may affect more than unit especially if flooding is the cause.

Condominium

A condo is a single unit in a larger building. The best advantage to opting to invest in condos is their low maintenance factor. In addition to this, the exterior of the house or building will be taken care of. All you have to take care of is interior of the house

Other advantages:

- Amazing recreational things to do such as swimming, gym, etc.

Disadvantages:

- Will be sharing your living space with a lot of people

- Privacy is limited.

Tips for Beginner Investors in Rental Real Estate

Here is some excellent advice for people considering this as their stream of passive income:

1. Look at real estate rentals as a long-term investment. This will provide you with higher returns on your investment.

2. Start with a ready-to-move-in property. Places that need work are ideal for those with some experience in property investment. Renovations usually take longer than expected and cost more than anticipated.

3. When it comes to negotiating and purchasing, seek the experience of a professional real estate agent. He or she will guide you in the right direction.

4. Conduct your research on the property market before your first purchase. Read up on trends, how to manage property rentals, etc.

5. Consider being an owner-occupant as it comes with lesser responsibilities of being a landlord.

6. Make sure your credit score is good before looking at getting a loan.

7. Investigate all your financing options before pulling the trigger, like hard money loans and real estate syndication.

8. Start to network with contractors, suppliers, realtors and other investors and landlords. They might be of great help in the future.

It is recommended to be business-minded and to approach real estate investing like you are running a business. Take a business course if necessary to learn about the financial terminology, accounting and financial statements and principles of building wealth.

Do have an exit strategy in mind. You don't want to focus on your real estate investment plan failing but as the future is inevitable for no one, having a plan B will help minimize potential loss. Ideally selling your property will help you with that.

How Much Money Can You Make?

To be honest, this really depends on how much money you have invested and how many properties you have rented out. But an average is $50,000 a year, now you can probably make more than that, but it requires you to have more properties. But the best part about this method is that you will have sellable investments, meaning you will most likely not lose money, simply sell it.

In all your excitement you may be tempted to head out and look for the first available property that looks profitable and sit back and wait for the rental income to come in. The reality of real estate investment is that it takes time for things to fall into place. It takes time to find the right property and to make it yours to rent then finally. Also, there are a lot of rules and legal matters to go through before you get started on this. The best way to avoid making mistakes is to be aware of what they can be and to not exercise them. Connect with other landlords. Their knowledge and experience can be used to better your chances of not facing any adversities in your real estate investments.

Options Trading

Just like the previous chapter, this chapter will also be a bit "theoretical," so please read it a couple of times if you don't understand it fully at first try. Now, there are two types of options trading—one is call options, and the other is put options. Thus, in this chapter, we will be going through the two options and will discuss how they work. Without further ado, let us get into it!

Call Options

To explain call options, we will be using an analogy. Let's say you work in the automotive industry. You know the ins and outs of it. You also know exactly how much a specific car is worth and if it will go up in price or not in future, now you get some insiders news that the 1996 corvettes will be going up in prices in 6 months from now. Just like anyone in the interest of making some profits you start looking for a 1996 corvette, and lo and behold— you find the perfect example of one for sale.

Now, it will cost you $20,000 to buy one, and you only have $5,000 to spare. But you do know that you will be getting a bonus in 6 months for $20,000 which will cover the cost of the car, but unfortunately, it will be too late by then as the prices will go up. So, what you do is this: offer the seller $5,000 as a down payment for the car. You will tell the seller that you will have the full amount of $20,000 in 6 months from now for the car until then you will take the car off the market, and in 6 months you will buy it for a fixed price of $20,000. If you can't fulfill the cost of the car in the six months' time, the seller keeps the vehicle and the $5,000 and if you do have the funds ready in 6 months you can buy the car for the fixed price of $20,000.

Let's now talk about how this would work in the stock trading market, for example, if a stock is trading at $10 and you think it will go up to $20, what you can do is buy $15 "call option" for $0.10. If your predictions where right and the stock did go up to $20, then you could buy the stock at $15 even if the stock is at $20 netting you a profit of $4.90. But like in the analogy above there is a time limit, so let us say the stock didn't go up until $20 by the time you had predicted it to go up then you are out $0.10 cents, and the seller keeps the $0.10.

Put Options

Now, we will be using the same analogy for put option as we did for the call option. So, let us say you ended up buying the Corvette for $20,000, to keep yourself and the car safe you decide to buy insurance at $1,000 for a year's coverage. In case of an accident or theft, the insurance company will cover your losses. Let's just say a year goes by and nothing happens to your car. You are happy that nothing happened, and you bought the insurance for your peace of mind, and the insurance company is satisfied that nothing happened to your car and they get to keep the $1,000.

In another example, let's say your car has been damaged and it will cost you $4,000 to fix the damages. You decide to use your insurance to cover your losses, and the insurance covers your losses as promised. In the final example, your car gets stolen. Now you are out $20,000! Don't worry. The coverage is more than happy to cover your loss of $20,000 as it happened within the year. You see, the insurance company doesn't mind paying out $4,000 or $20,000 for your damages when you only paid $1,000 as it is getting the $1,000 premium from multiple people. They would need to pay out $20,000 in that year, but they got $1,000 premium from 100 people, which means they made $80,000 profit in a year.

Now let's use put option in a trading scenario. So if a stock is floating around $15 per share and you have a feeling that it will drop down to $10. As a safety net, you could buy a $12.50 put option for $0.10. If the stock drops down to $10, you will still have the possibility of selling it at $12.50 even if the stock is at $10. Netting you a profit of $2.40, on the other hand, this would leave the person at a loss of $2.40 who sold you the "put option." Now if the stock never drops down to $10 in a certain amount of time and the "put" expires then the put buyer is out $0.10, and the seller keeps the $0.10 as profit.

It is a gamble.

You are now well educated on options trading, and you know that it can be a gamble. Therefore, I would not recommend making this your sole income as the cash flow is unpredictable. Exercise this method on the side to make money.

How Much Money Can You Make?

Just like stocks, you cannot put a number. People have made millions of dollars from options trading, and some have lost millions of dollars on options trading so like I said there is no fixed rate of pay you will be getting but also there is no cap on how much you can make.

Now before you go and try out your luck in this, please remember to know what kind of risk you are putting yourself into. There is no guarantee that you will make money or lose money, it is a gamble. For you to make it less of a chance, find out everything about the stocks you will be buying, know if it will be going down or up in price and then make your call. Just remember to make this your side income stream rather than your sole income as it could lead you to lose some money if not all. So, remember, practice with smaller amounts of money and have the discipline to stop when you feel like you are going into deep.

Shopify Dropshipping

Now, we are going to be talking about a method that can be quite lucrative if done right—as the title says, we will be discussing dropshipping. Now, what is dropshipping? Well, to put it in simple terms, dropshipping is a business model where you are going to act as the "middle man." Thus, mainly, what you are going to do is find a product from a supplier at a meager price. After you see a cheap product, you will then use Shopify to create an online store wherein you can sell your products. The best part about this method is that you will be provided with photos of the products by the supplier—so you don't even have to see the products in person.

After you have found a product and created, you're the store. You will then hike up the price of the product which you are getting for really cheap, then find people who would be interested in your products and cater to them. Once they purchase the product from you, you will then go to your supplier and buy it for the meager price which you are offered and directly ship it to the buyer without you even touching the product leaving you with some profit in your pocket.

In a nutshell, that's what the whole dropshipping business entails. Since you now have an idea of what the dropshipping business, we will talk about how to start this business from the ground up, we will go through how to set up you're store to how to market your products and everything in the middle. This chapter should indeed teach you everything you need to know about dropshipping and to take your business to the next level. Now, to begin with, we will cover the essentials you need to start your dropshipping business.

Basics of Shopify

Now, first of all, I would like to say there are other websites like Shopify where you can start your online store. You don't need to use Shopify as your online store, but for simplicity and the popularity of Shopify, we will cover the upfront investment based on Shopify.

Like we discussed before, starting your online store you will need to find a supplier who can provide you with products for cheap, and also can ship out the products for really cheap anywhere in the world. Since we have gotten that out of the way, we will now have to discuss how much the startup cost be for you to start your very own dropshipping business.

To begin with the cheaper investment, you will first have to come up with a store name which isn't taken and to also buy a domain name for your website. To make your site look professional, you need to have a proper domain name. Luckily purchasing a domain name is cheap, it should only cost you $11 to 18 a year for your unique domain name. So after you come up with a store name and a domain name which isn't taken, it would be now time to sign up for Shopify. Even though Shopify comes with a 14-day free trial, for you to fulfill an order, you will have to sign up for a paid membership with Shopify. Shopify offers three packages, which include the following:

- Basic Shopify package (USD 29.99) a month

- Shopify package ($79.99) a month

- Advanced Shopify package ($299.99) a month

Now, there is an option to buy these subscriptions upfront for the whole year, which would save you some money overall but that is entirely up to you.

So now comes the time to decide, which one do you sign up for? So, let's go through all three and find the right package for you. Now for 99% of the people starting their dropshipping business, you don't need to get the advanced package, in future when you have made your business more profitable and you have many more orders to fulfill then you can consider upgrading to the advanced package. But for now pick between the basic Shopify package or the Shopify package, if you feel the whole burn model out and you don't want to invest so much into it, then you can quickly start with the cheapest package. Now, if you really want to make this your full-time business and you have some extra cash to spare, then I recommend getting the Shopify package.

There are some useful benefits to upgrading, as compared to the basic package the Shopify package has lower credit card rates. Although the prices might be small, it will still add up once you start making a full-time income out of it. Another great tool the Shopify package offers is that it lets you create gift cards. As you know by now, you need to provide incentives to your customers to sell more. So providing these incentives could add up and make you more money, but it doesn't matter which one you get started with as long as you have a platform to sell your products. So it really depends on what you like and which one fits your budget, so choose wisely.

So now for the housekeeping staff, you will need a logo for your Shopify store. You should ideally get it done professionally by hiring someone on fiverr.com. The logo will not cost you more than USD 25 to get started. Again, if you're feeling out the business or you don't have enough money to invest then get a free logo by using websites like canva.com. Regardless of it being free or not, you will need a logo.

Now, to sum up, the total costs of getting started with dropshipping using Shopify.

- Shopify package $29.99 or $79.99 USD

- Domain name $ 11 to $18 USD

- Logo $0.00 to $25

Approximately, to get started with you're the dropshipping business it will cost you $40.99 and USD 29.99 every month after the first month, for the cheapest option or $122.99 and $79.99 every month after the first for the most expensive option. Regardless the startup should be quite affordable for anyone.

Now, let us cover more housekeeping stuff for your Shopify business to flourish. You defiantly need to make your website look professional. Luckily Shopify provides you with free websites themes which will make your site look amazing. Now, be sure to communicate with any customer inquiries or complaints. As you will be creating your brand and company, everything from dealing with fulling an order and to complete orders will be your responsibility. Making an email address specific to your store/brand is imperative. That is all the housekeeping you need to worry about to make you're store look presentable and professional.

So this is all you need to know to make your Shopify store, now we have to discuss how to find a profitable niche where you can sell and make money and also how to properly market your product to get sales.

Profitable Niches

Since you now have an idea of what it takes to get you to store up and to run, it would be far the time to discuss how to find a niche where you can sell into. Now for those who don't know what a slot is, as lots something which is a part of a product or a service. So an example of a slot would be car racing, people who enjoy cars and like to see car races they are a part of a niche.

So your goal should be to find a niche which doesn't have a lot of completion and to sell products to the people part of that niche in order to make some sales. There are two ways to find a niche which would be profitable for you:

- Amazon

- Facebook/Instagram pages

Now, I have used these to websites/pages to find one of the most profitable niches there are for drop shipping. So to find a profitable niche off of Amazon is quite simple, go to the best sellers on Amazon. Look at the list carefully and see a slot which is selling the most, so for example, if there are five iPhone cases on the top sellers' list then the chances are iPhone cases/electronics have a demand, which would mean that this might be a potential niche to get into. Remember anything that sells well on Amazon will sell anywhere, which uncles you're storing so find products on Amazon.

Let us talk about Facebook/ Instagram pages, have you ever stumbled upon one of the weirdest pages online thinking "man how do people like or a following for this." Well, pages like these are gold mines, since these pages are super-niche and have practically no products for sale for their specific niche. The people on those pages are waiting to spend money on outcomes related to that niche. If you find a niche which has a lot of following (around 200k followers) and it is super niche, then chances are there are less competition and more money to be made by you. So with that being said, remember that you can really find unusual, profitable niches using these two techniques listed in this chapter for your dropshipping business. Now it is time to talk about advertising your products.

Advertising

Now, there are a lot of advertising methods to be used we will specifically be learning about Facebook advertising. Since Facebook is the hardest to cover, yet it is the cheapest way to promote your products. So let us dive into the world of Facebook advertising.

There are a lot of people on Facebook around 2 billion people, so finding someone who would be interested in your product won't be so hard. Facebook advertising has been used from small dropshipping companies to big companies like Nike etc. there is no denying the fact that Facebook is the cheapest most effective way to advertise your products. Just like anything, there is a process and a technique you need to go through to make a successful Facebook ad campaign. The first thing would be to create an ads account on Facebook.

Once you have created your Facebook ads account, you will then have to link your store pixel to your account. This is so important, here is the reason why once you add you're the pixel to your Facebook ads manager, it will then collect data for your website and product. The pixel will collect data's like, what kind of people are watching, clicking and buying your products which would mean better insights for you to use as a marketing tool. As this would help you determine different people or websites to target too. So after you have created you're Facebook ads page and have managed to connect your pixel to your ads page, it time to start advertising. Here are some things you need to take care of before you start advertising:

- Finding products similar to yours

- Finding Facebook ads related to your products

- Targeting a specific age group and country

So I know there are only three things to worry about, but trust me these things are enormous for your success in this business.

So let's start off with the first step finding similar products to yours. Once you first make your ad campaign, it will ask you to do is to write down companies or websites similar to yours. What we will do is go online and start looking for products for sale identical to ours. For example, if I am selling a phone I will look up "phones for sale" then I want you to click on all the websites which sell your products. So in this hypothetical scenario, I would be clicking through Apple, Nokia etc., so after you do that I want you to write down all the websites which are related to your niche or product that you are going to be selling.

After you have all the top websites, I want you to search up the sites which were similar to you, and find their Facebook pages. Once you have done that check to see if their Facebook likes are over 500,000 and if so, you have found a page which can be used to advertise your product. What Facebook will do with this information on your ads campaign is that I will promote your products to people interested in that page. So let us get back to my hypothetical scenario—if I am selling a phone and I add Apple to my targeted Facebook advertisement, it will then specifically target people who are interested in Apple products. So find a product with a Facebook page that has over 500k followers, then finally advertise it to the people involved in that page.

Since you now have the keywords and the specific people you will be advertising your products too it is now time to create a professional advertisement. I will assume that most of the people here haven't created a Facebook ad, for people who have created Facebooks ads will know that it is essential that you have a fantastic and display. Some of you might have heard the phrase "if it ain't broke don't fix it" Meaning that there are big companies making millions if not billions of dollars using Facebook ad and a simple yet effective template, so it is recommended you copy what they are doing as it will yield you the most results.

So, if you did you're researching online like suggested, you should have started to see the websites advertising on your Facebook. The next time you see one, jot down notes on how they exactly advertise their products. Once you have thoughtfully examined the advertisement, I want you to use a similar template to create yours from photo to caption. Trust me it saves a lot of money on trial and error.

Once you have analyzed ads on Facebook, it will be no time to create your very one. Now, before you start your first ads campaign on Facebook, it will ask you to put an age range on your advertisement. So if you are going to be selling a phone case, for example, I would probably set the age range around 20-to 50 as most of the people. Since most <, 20 years old won't be buying one by themselves and anyone over >50 won't either. Our goal is to narrow down the audience, so we can target the specific people and get the most sales out of it.

When picking out the county or region to advertise it to, I would recommend you promote it to U.S.A only if your budget is small. Most of your buyers will be coming from united states, so it is not necessary to advertise it into other countries on the beginning. Now, if you want to promote it to more countries you then I would recommend picking out first world countries like Canada, U.K., as they will have more consumers for you as compared to third world countries.

How Much Money Can You Make?

So the answer is genuinely infinite since it is your brand and you're not affiliated with anyone you can make as much money as you want. Let's take Kylie Jenner for instance, she started her dropshipping business with Shopify and now is worth $900 million. The sky is the limit, so if your goal is to become a millionaire or even a billionaire with Shopify, you can just put your mind to it.

Now before you start trying your luck with Shopify, work and understand every aspect of this chapter. Especially the advertisement portion of the chapter, make sure that you have an idea on how to drive traffic to your store. Because if you don't, then you won't be getting a lot of sales. Also, remember to not invest more money than you can, in the beginning, you don't need a lot to get started.

Amazon FBA

If you haven't heard of Amazon by now, chances are you are living under a rock. Jeff Bezos, who is worth over $150 billion, founded the company in the early 90s as a storefront for books. Fast forward to now where Amazon sells anything you could want—from toilet papers to full television sets, Amazon has got you covered.!

How Amazon FBA works is simple. First, you find a product from a cheap supplier and then sell it to people at a markup price on Amazon— leaving you with some profit in your pocket.

Now, if you're wondering, what does the FBA stand for? It stands for Fulfillment by Amazon. Think of Amazon as similar to Shopify, except two things; first you will be selling your products on Amazon, and second, you will have to ship your products to their warehouse before you can start fulfilling orders. So you will have to find a supplier and ship the products to the nearest Amazon warehouse, so the upfront investment would be a little bit higher as compared to Shopify. To break it down, here is the approximate cost of a startup:

- Buying products in bulk for cheap $1000 — USD 3000

- If you sell more than 40 items a month, you will have to pay $39.99

On the lower end, you can get started for USD 1000 to USD 3000 plus $39.99 a month if you sell more than 40 products. There is also a charge per shipped product, but that will be decided out your payout.

So even though there is a bigger upfront investment, there are still a lot of advantages, for instance, you will be promoting your product on a website which already gets a bunch of free traffic. Meaning that you will have more success, in the beginning, to sell your products as compared to other methods. Another great benefit would be that there is no need to worry out creating a storefront as Amazon would be your storefront.

So, without further ado let's get into the specifics of starting your business from the ground up using Amazon fab. Mostly, you will have to figure out three things before you begin to advertise on this platform, which are:

1. Profitable product

2. Finding a supplier

3. Advertising your product

Profitable Product

Now, to find a profitable product you have to remember two things. First find out what is selling on Amazon, second check the competition on Amazon. You need to make sure that there is a demand for the product and secondly, there is not a lot of game of that product on Amazon as it can make it difficult to sell online. Hence, making sure that these two things are in check is imperative for you to the success on this platform as well as to remember that finding a profitable product depends on uniqueness. Let's take the fidget spinner, for example, although unique it offered its users something to fidget with hence "fidget spinner." It helped people to get rid of any "fidgety" feeling they might have so to speak and also was a fun little game of the children, so although it isn't necessary to find a product like a fidget spinner it is essential to dive into a profitable niche.

To find a profitable niche, there are a couple of ways to do so, one of them using Amazon. So for some that might know, Amazon is the biggest e-commerce website of this day and age, meaning whatever sells on Amazon will most likely sell anywhere in the word. So to find a profitable product or niche could be very easy on Amazon, the first thing you would want to do is check the best sellers list on Amazon. This will give you a guide of what is selling online right now, the second check to see how many niche specific products are for sale online. So if you check the best sellers list and you see five examples of an iPhone case on there, the chances are that iPhone and electronics accessories is a great niche to get into.

One thing to remember though, most of the products on the best sellers list already have a competitive price which would be hard for beginners to beat. So what you want to do is find a sub-niche in that category, so, for instance, you have decided to use the electronic accessories as your niche. What you will do is find a "keyword" or a niche which has more than 6 products in the top 100,000 best sellers list on Amazon and has less than 1,000 results. So if you look up "iPhone phone case glitter" as your keyword—and if you check to see top 6 products are rated at 100,000 on the best sellers list and the results are less than a 1,000, then this would be a great product and a niche to get into.

Since everything is getting so competitive these days online, it is essential to find these super-niche products if you want to be successful from the get-go in this business. Thus making sure you see this super-niche on Amazon is recommended before you go ahead and invest your money on a product which may or may not sell, so if you want to save your money and rather earn more money, then do your research and find those "sub-niche" as there is a lot of money to be made there and just like always do your research.

Finding a Supplier

Finding a supplier for your Amazon FBA business quite easy as compared to Shopify, there are three ways of finding you're the supplier for Amazon for 1. Ali expresses 2. Warehouse 3. Big sales. As you can see, you have a lot of options as to where you could find your products—let us talk about each method.

So same suppliers most dropshippers use, using websites like Ali express can help you to make money online without any hesitations. The beauty about Ali express it that it has about 99.9% of the things you want to sell or own, they have it and that too for a bargain of a price. So it is a shame not to use these websites to find products and to resell it at a markup on Amazon. Now the couple of things to remember, most of the products on Ali express aren't of the highest of the quality. So to find a product which would sell and help you make money for a long time, there are a couple of things you can to ensure that you are not robbed of you're an investment. The first you need to do is find the right supplier, so to find the right supplier here is two things to check for.

The first thing is review's check the sellers' review on Ali-Express, if the review is below a 4.5 out of 5 then chances are the seller is not reliable or has excellent quality products hence needs to be discarded from your supplier list. The second thing to take note of would be to see how many orders the supplier has fulfilled. If a supplier has fulfilled more than 500 orders, then there is a high chance that the supplier is reliable and has excellent quality products. So, if these two things check out, then you can start to order from them.

Warehouse

Using warehouses nearby you to find cheap supplies for your product can be a great alternative compared to using the traditional way of Ali-express. Now, most people use places like Costco to find cheap supplies in bulk and sell it off on Amazon. So for you to a warehouse can be a great option as it can save you on shipping cost and check out the products in person before you decide to purchase it.

Now, there are some pros and cons to this method of finding supplies. The first one would be the fact that it is hard to find great warehouses or great product supplies using this method. So even though Costco is used for some people for their Amazon for business, it still has some flaws like the way it is packaged. Sometimes Costco packages the product in such a manner that it is hard to resell it. But, if you do find products in Costco to resell then do it! As the products will yield you a lot of profits.

The second problem using this method would be to find warehouses that sell your products, so here is the thing—finding a warehouse that sells your products besides Costco can be a challenge to see when you first start your Amazon for. So if you do find a warehouse which does sell the products that you are looking for, then chances are it would be a cheaper option as compared to Ali express. Ideally, if you can use other warehouses in your county to find products, as it can be a more affordable option.

Finally, I would like to talk about utilizing big sales which can be used to find products which you can resell. Utilizing black Friday, Cyber Monday to save money on the products that you want or need. Luckily, you can use these sales to bulk up on your products which you can sell later on Amazon at a low price.

For example, a product which would cost you around $75 on Amazon would be going for $35 on that specific day. So what you can do is buy the product in bulk at the price of $35 and then wait a couple of weeks and sell it on Amazon for $65 undercutting your competition, which would mean more sales for you! But, the problem with this method is that it isn't a recurring as the other two methods. Although it can be used as a great tool, it is indeed short-lived so capitalize on it as much as you can.

Hopefully, this helped you figure out how to find the right supplier for your product and business. Just remember that either of these three methods would work make sure that you are doing everything in your power to save money on the supplies, so make sure to pick the cheapest supplier every time you have to restock your inventory.

Advertising

Now to make sure everyone is on the same page, even though Amazon offers us such a fantastic source of free traffic. It is still recommended to invest in some paid traffic. You have to take into consideration the fact that Amazon has so many products for sale on its website that sometimes it just becomes hard to showcase every single product on sale to people.

So to get some sales on your Amazon fab account you might have to invest in some paid advertising, now there are two methods you can use to advertise your products. The first one would be to utilize Amazon's inbuilt tool to start marketing the second one would be to use YouTube's to advertise you're the product.

So to begin with we will talk about using Amazon's inbuilt advertising tool, it is quite simple to use and effective, look up keywords related to your product and start advertising accordingly. Then you set up a daily budget similar to Facebook's way of advertising, and there you have your Amazon's advertising.

The second one can be done for free, but there is a trick involved. Now, most of the you-tubers use Amazon's very own Affiliate Marketing program to make money, what you can do is ask them to promote your products on YouTube which would help them earn some affiliate commission and make you some money.

Finally, you can use Facebooks paid advertising platform to advertise your very own products.

How Much Money Can You Make?

So, of course, everyone wants to know how much money they can make, well to begin with I would like to say a lot! Yes, you can make a lot of money doing this business model. But there is a catch if you want to make loads of money this business can't be passive in the beginning. There will be a lot of trial and errors before you can indeed make this business passive. Now the good part is that once you get the ball rolling, it takes little to no effort to upkeep the company, so if you follow everything written in this book correctly, you can make anywhere to $1,000 to $100,000.

Now I did say a lot of money, not infinite money, unlike Shopify there is a cap on the income, unfortunately you can't expect to make more than 2 million a year from this business model just because it isn't a brand you personally created so to grow it even farther than that could be a task. So, if you want to become a millionaire, you technically can and if you're going to make an extra $1,000 a month you most definitely can as it is entirely up to you to decide. Either way, there is some hard work needed in the beginning to start earning money.

So to conclude this chapter I would like to remind you a couple of things before you get started on your Amazon for business, remember that it takes time and effort to begin this business, but once you get the ball rolling, you can make infinite amounts of money with it. Remember that for you make money in this business you need to find the right supplier who will help you to with delivering high-quality products to your clients. Secondly, you will have to make sure that you adverse your product the right way by utilizing paid advertising tools provided. But the main thing to worry about is to make sure that you indeed have a winning product. Remember it takes time and effort to find a winning product, and with the information provided in this book, you can find one. So keep trying and eventually it will materialize into the business that you are looking for.

Selling Merchandise

Now, you might have heard of this topic before—but if not, let me explain to you on how this works. Selling merchandise is merely selling a t-shirt with a distinctive logo to a client. It could be anything like shoes, pillow cases, etc. However, most of the time, this is used for selling t-shirts. How this works is simple—specific websites or apps allow you to add any logo that your heart desires and sell it to customers. It is similar to dropshipping since you don't have to see the products, and they ship out directly to your customers.

This method is probably the most trending right now regarding making money online since it is so new you can make money with it rather quickly. Now there are a couple of things we need to take care of before you can go ahead and start your very own business of selling merchandise. Now, there are a lot of platforms you can use to start you're very personal such as Amazon merchandise, Redbubble, and your very own Shopify. It is entirely up to you which website you use to get started with as it is entirely up to you, and luckily the start-up cost for all is very cheap and reasonably affordable, so you don't need to worry about investing a lot of money into it. All you need to worry about is the monthly payment of websites and the cost to get a logo design done, that's all.

So with that said, here are three things you need to take care of before you can start your business of selling merchandise. 1. Find a niche 2. Make an Instagram/ Facebook page 3. Advertising. So all these things are essential if you want to be successful in this business, so without further ado, let us get into it.

Finding a Niche

Finding a niche is very important for you actually to make this business profitable, think about it? Why would someone want to buy your t-shirt, it is merely a t-shirt. Whereas, if you make a meme t-shirt everyone who is a fan of memes would be interested in buying your product. It is essential that you find a niche you would want to sell into.

Now, there are a lot of niches to get into. Your job is to find one where you can sell t-shirts relating to the niche. Now there are a lot of examples of this, but I will use one for the readers so they can get a better idea, so if you ever stumble upon fitness gurus or fitness channels on YouTube these guys solely sell use these methods to make and distribute it to the buyers, since they have a following large people want to buy from them.

The beauty about finding a niche in this business model is that you can make any topic or niche profitable business. So if you like bowling, you can create cool bowling logos and sell it to people who would be interested in bowling. As long as you have a cool logo, you can sell your t-shirts. Also, you need to get traffic on you're the page, but we will get into that topic later on in this chapter.

So listen—you don't need to find a specific niche. You can enter any slot your heart desires and sell it on there as long as the logo looks cool and you have people in that niche aware of your t-shirt or any merchandise for that matter.

Making an Instagram/Facebook Page

Now, once you have found out which niche you will be getting into it would be no time to make an Instagram and a Facebook page on that subject. Now, most people don't talk about this, but making a niche specific page and growing it to a big following can get you a bunch of sales. As this would be targeted advertising, you will first gain people's trust by posting amazing photos and logs on your page, so people follow and once it grows out to be a more prominent page, you can then start selling mechanize to them, and it will sell.

There are a couple of ways to grow your Instagram page, one them would be to buy followers online. But that isn't effective if you want to improve your brand and get more sales, remember it is much better to have 1,000 followers active than 10,000 followers inactive. Our goal is to make an Instagram page which will help you make money, not boost your ego. Now to organically grow your Instagram page here are the top 5 things to do:

1. Be active on your account.

2. Follow and unfollow.

3. Post-high-quality photos.

4. Get paid promotions from bigger pages.

5. Join an engagement group.

So the first thing we will be covering would be being active on Instagram, being active on Instagram means that you are continually liking and commenting on photos and videos on Instagram, what this does is gets you to account out there and visible to the people who might be interested in following you. Once you start liking and commenting on the photos and videos on a more prominent Instagram page, often you will begin to notice your channel is getting free publicity and people will start to follow you. So make sure you are doing this religiously every day to grow your Instagram page.

The second thing would be to use a method known as "follow unfollow." Essentially what your goal with this method is to follow as many active users as possible, and then unfollow after three days or so. There are some online tools which will take care of this process for you, so you can either go that route, or you can go the other direction and do this manually. If you do go manually make sure to write down their names so you can unfollow them after three days or so. This technique still works to gain quick followers in a hurry, make sure that you are utilizing it, especially in the beginning.

The third method would be to make sure you provide users with some high-quality photos, and this is crucial for your Instagram to grow. If your page is about camping and outdoor activities, and you post landscape photos they can't be of and quality. You need to make sure you have high-quality images, and you can use other Instagram pages photos which are of high quality but always make sure to tag them on your post. One company who has done this successfully is outdoor_hack, they are a Shopify based account—and even though they don't have any photos taken specially for them, they still have managed to grow and make money. So if you are looking for some inspiration, I would check that page out on Instagram.

The fourth thing you can do would be to use bigger pages online to promote your page. How this works is that you pay them money for a 24 hour or 12-hour shout out, most of the time they post it on their story or feed. This works great if you have some money to invest, merely getting shout-outs from bigger pages can help you grow your page quite rapidly.

Now, finally, we will talk about engagement groups. This is the method most people use to take their page/ pages to the next level. This method will make your page skyrocket in followers and of course more sales for your merchandise business. So what an engagement group is that is a group of pages similar in size, what everyone in this group will do is whenever you post a photo they will like and comment on it the photo, and you will also have to love others photos and comment on them.

Every engagement group has different rules, but most of them pre-decide when everyone is going to post online. Everyone in the group has to like and comment on that specific post within the allotted time period of typically 30 minutes, and If you don't follow the rules, you will be kicked out of the group, period. So make sure to follow the rules, and finally, make sure to follow all the four steps above so you can actually utilize this tool correctly and get the most out of it.

Now, most of my readers might be wondering, why did I ramble on growing a niche based Instagram account. Here is the reason why look most people won't tell you this, but this business model won't work correctly if you don't have a niche based Instagram/Facebook page. So if you want to make money out of this business model, having a niche page with a big following is a big part of you're the success. Now, this takes time if you want to get quick sales fast you will have to advertise your product.

Advertising

Now, once you have created a Facebook page, you can use that page to utilize Facebooks advertising services to promote your products. It is the exact same process as the one described in chapter 6 so make sure to check that out. But we again come back to Instagram advertising to make money, it just works so much better than any other method.

Instagram, as I said before, is a great place to advertise your products, especially for the merchandise business since it is such a niche based one, so if your goal is to get quick sales on your page, you can use this method. When we advise on Instagram most of the time, you will use a technique called "Instagram influencer."

Similar to promoting your page for more followers you will find an Instagram page which is related to your topic which also has a big following, then you will get a paid shout-out from them and see the sales come in. People who are in the business of selling merchandise online can say this is one of the fastest ways of getting sales. There are three things you need to take care of before you start advertising on an Instagram page.

- Finding the right influencer

- Making sure they don't have any BOTs

- Knowing how much engagement are they getting

As you know by now, in order to get sales and make money you need to make sure you are promoting you're the product to the right audience. Hence, you cannot promote a fitness shirt on a page that is about global warming. Make sure the page you decide to encourage on is about what you are trying to promote.

Just a little side note, make sure whichever page you choose has over 300k followers. Now, this depends on the niche to niche, but this a good rule of thumb to follow when picking out your influencer.

Now finding an account in your niche with over 300k followers is tremendous, but what's their engagement like? The truth is some pages have 'bots'—meaning, they have bought followers for their page. There are a couple of ways to find out if that's the case or not, but if someone is not getting at least 5-10% of their followers like their post meaning if they have 100k followers and they are not getting at least 5-10k likes, then the chances are their follows have been bought.

So in order to get a shout from these Instagram pages, you will have to message them directly saying something along the lines of wanting a shout-out. Once you guys have decided on a price, you can start to promote your product on their page once they receive the payment. One thing to remember is there is no need to get a 24-hour shout out for a product ad. All of the followers on the page will see your advertisement within the 12 hours, so no need to advertise it longer than you should.

How Much Money Can You Make?

Now, this totally depends on you, but you can make as much as a $1,000 to as much as you want the sky is truly the limit. Like Shopify, you can make a lot of money with this method, make sure you have a niche brand and also make sure to grow it as big as you can. You can become a millionaire if not a billionaire with this method, but if you want to make some extra cash on the side, it would be very easy to do so with this method.

So remember to follow everything that is said in this chapter if you want to start earning some cash. The biggest secret revealed is to grow your very own Instagram pages, this is something that isn't talked about so much. Creating logos and other aspects of the business is very easy to do but if you want to grow your business and take it to the next level makes sure to create and improve your

Instagram account as quickly as possible. Also, make sure to pick a niche which you have interest and passion for it will more likely grow bigger for you as compared to others.

Self-Publishing

This business model isn't talked about so much, but it is very lucrative. Self-publishing began with Amazon back in around 2010, and it has now used by many people to make money online. Some people say that self-publishing has died and that it doesn't work—but I will be the first one to tell you that it is alive and well. Now, there are a lot of online self-publishing websites that can be used to make money online—but today, we will only be talking about Amazon's self-publishing platform, as it is the most lucrative to get into.

Now what the self-publishing business entails is this, you first write a book and then Amazon will publish it for you on its website. It will also give you 75% of the royalties on the e-book version and 60% on the paperback version. Meaning that you will get paid 75% of the listed price of the book or 60%, which will depend on the version of the book. Now with that being said, this business is still very lucrative, and you can easily make some good money on the side.

In order for you to make sure this business is successful and you can get the most out of it, you will need to make sure that you have these main points in check. Those points are 1. Book creation & book-length 2. Book cover & formatting 3. Niche & keywords. So in today's chapter, we will go through all three of these aspects to make sure that you're on track to making money off of this method.

Book Creation & Book Length

So, as you know by now that you need to make sure that you have a book in order to sell it. There are two ways you can go about getting this done, first of all, you can write it yourself. Secondly, you can hire a ghostwriter to write it for you. Either works, but its highly recommend you get some professional help and work with a ghostwriter, one of the best companies you can get your book is written with would be to use a website called ewritersolutions.com. now with that being said, you need to remember the fact that you can write your own book, so if you don't have enough money to invest in hiring a ghostwriter then you can easily do it yourself.

Now to touch bases on the book-length, most people these days don't want a book which is going to be over 150-200 pages. So if you're getting the book written for over 40,000 words then you are doing something wrong, with that said an ideal amount of word for your book would be anywhere from 8,000 on the short side to 15,000 on the more extended hand. But that's just a rough number it can be as long as 40,000 words.

Book Cover & Formatting

Now, on the other hand, you need to make sure you're book cover looks professional as it will help you sell your book. So unless you are an experienced graphic designer, then I would suggest you hire someone to make a fantastic cover for you. You can use websites like fiverr.com to find great book cover designers for you. Since my recommendation would be to have both a paperback version and a Kindle version of the book, then those two have two separate covers. But it should not require you to spend more than $20 for getting both the cover and the book.

You will also need to get your book correctly formatted and ready before you put it up on Amazon's website. Again, if you're a professional editor/designer then skip this step if not then make sure to hire a professional for this job. There are a lot of people on Fiverr who can help you with this, they will format the book to fit kindle and paperback requirements by Amazon publishing platform so don't worry about that. It should again cost you less than $20 to get this done.

Niche & Keywords

So finally the main reason why your book will sell, this topic which needs to be discussed in detail. If you're niche or keywords are not in the order they should be then chances are your book won't sell. So if you're looking to write a book on a specific niche you need to make sure that the book will sell—and in order to find out if it will, you will then need to make sure that the book will sell you need to make sure the niche is profitable.

So in order to find a profitable niche what you can do is this, the first thing you need to do is go onto Amazon.com. Secondly, I want you to search for the main keyword of the book you will be writing. So for example, if the topic of the book is meditation then search up meditation on Amazon, make sure that the search is on kindle store if it isn't then the chances are it won't give you accurate data. After you have done that I want you to go through the top six books, if the top six books on mediation have the Amazon bestseller rank lower than 100,000 then that niche is profitable and would make you money.

Once you have found your niche to write on, and everything else like the book cover and the formatting is good to go, it would now finally be the time to pick out the seven keywords for you're a book on Amazon. Now, the reason behind this is so that Amazon can showcase your books in those top seven keywords whenever someone searches the keywords you have inputted. So it is not only, but without the right keywords, people won't see your books on Amazon which would mean no sales.

Now to find the right keywords you need to keep in mind these factors, first, you need to make sure that all the keywords you pick follow the same rules of having the top 4-6 books under 100k on the Amazon's bestseller list, if not then it is not a right keyword to get into. So for my books to sell, I like to use a method known as "pyramid method," what is entails merely is have 1 big essential world 2 medium keyword and 4 small keywords. So a big keyword would be any keyword with a search result of over 10k, the medium would be any search result of between 10k and 5k and the small keywords would be everything under 5k.

Now to find these keywords can become a challenge, but there are a couple of ways to get this done. You can use a software called as "KDP Rocket." It simply finds all the medium and the smaller keywords by you putting in the larger keywords. So for example, if you type in meditation, it will show you all the keywords with the size of the keyword and the book in it with the Amazon's best seller rank in it. So if you want to make your life easier, use KDP Rocket—if not, it can be done manually by simply inputting every keyword you can think about regarding meditation on the search engine of Amazon, like "meditation for beginners" etc. even though it is a long process, it can be done for free.

So what we just discussed right now was only to get your book up and ready to go, now we have to talk about how to market and advertise in order to get sales. Currently, there are three things we need to do in order to make money with this business.

1. Free promo

2. Collecting reviews

3. AMS advertising

Free Promo

So once you have uploaded you're book online it would be now time to start promoting your book. So one of the ways Amazon helps your book to get noticed is by either letting you have a sale on your e-book or to let you run a free promotion on your book, what we want to do is opt for 5-day free promotion. How Amazon works is the more downloads you get, the more likely Amazon will promote your book to others, and the best way to get more downloads is to use free promo. What this will do is let people download your book for free which will help your book get the more organic free promotion.

So make sure to promote your book by utilizing the free promo Amazon offers.

Collecting Reviews

Now, this is also very important, most people don't want to buy a product or a book if they don't have any reviews and most of the times it means positive reviews. So luckily there are some ways to collect these reviews which I will be revealing to you today, so the way I would go about it and would recommend his to do so by hiring a virtual assistant for Amazon self-publishing.

The way it works is quite simple, go on upwork.com and make a profile. Then I want you to post a job saying, looking for a virtual assistant for kindle publishing. The people will know what you are talking about exactly and will start messaging you, one thing to remember never pay more than $1.5 per review as it isn't worth it. After you have decided on a price you will now ask them to collect 20 to 40 reviews, and again this will depend on your budget but no less than 20 reviews. After your reviewer is ready to go tell him to collect it when your book is on the free promo for 5 days, that should be plenty of time for your reviewer to collect reviews for you.

Others ways you can collect more reviews is by merely adding you're the book on sights and Facebook pages which are related to book clubs. This should most definitely help you get some reviews, but don't use this as your only way to get reviews as it will leave you heartbroken so to speak.

AMS Advertising

Now, this method is not recommended for people who are on a budget as it is a paid advertising service provided by Amazon. But if you really want to take your Amazon self-publishing business to the next level, then you defiantly need to utilize this tool as it works great. Now there are some tips to make sure you're Amazon advertising doesn't go to waste.

The first thing would be to make sure that you have the right keywords, again I highly recommend using KDP Rocket as it will make a full updated list for your advertising keywords. Now, in order for your ads to be successful, you need to make sure that you have atlas 150 to 500 keywords for your ads. If you will be doing this manually then I highly recommend you write down every keyword you know related to your niche and use that to advertise, if you don't want to do so then you can use the automatic way of advertising. This method will only pick out the keywords for you, it, but it works so try that instead.

Another thing to remember is to set the cost per click at 0.25 cents, as you will merely start losing money if you don't do so. Finally, make sure to set the budget at $5 a day as that is all you need.

ACX

One more thing I would like briefly talk about would be to use "ACX," now "ACX" is a platform where you can turn your books into audiobooks. There are two ways you can go about it, either you pay a narrator a flat fee upfront or split the royalties 50/50. Now we won't get into too much of details, but if you want to supplement your income from Kindle publishing, you can do so by utilizing this method. Trust me it is super easy to find a narrator on this platform, and if you have the money to invest then pay the narrator upfront instead of splitting the royalties. As it will leave you with bigger royalty checks in your pocket at the end of the day, so definitely look into converting your book into an audiobook alongside your kindle versions and paperback.

How Much Money Can You Make?

Now, the good news is that this business model is the easiest to get started with. The bad news is that you can't make a lot of money out of this method—if you solely do self-publishing and nothing else, then you can expect to make no more than $10,000 a month. Which is still good, but don't expect to become a millionaire out of it. But if you want to make some extra side income, this is highly recommended.

Now, to conclude this chapter, I would just like to say that this method is the easiest method to get started with, you can start earning $1,000 a month in a matter of a month. But the only problem is that it isn't scalable as the others which could be a problem for some, with minimal to no effort this business can make some side income. So make sure to follow every tips and trick in this chapter to scale up truly your business, as these tips can't be found anywhere and they genuinely work.

Other Online Methods

So in all the previous chapters, we talked about the *major* ways to start earning some passive income—now, in this chapter, we will go through some quick, *minor* ways to make money online fast and now. To be honest, making money online isn't so hard, and it requires little to no effort on your end in terms of finding it.

According to one study, there used to be 10% of the world on the Internet—and now, around 46% of the world is online most of the time. Clearly, there is a lot of money to be made online. So far, in this book, we have discussed some of the bigger and more mainstream ways to make money. Those methods are great ways to make money online—but if you're a younger guy or girl with no money to invest in those major businesses, then this chapter will help you make some money quickly and without any upfront investment, so you can essentially make money starting *now*!

Before you start earning money with these websites and pages, I should let you know that none of these will be passive—so please be aware of that before you start using them. Please also know that these methods might work well in the short-term to make quick cash, but they can become way too time-consuming in the long run, so use them in a pinch or to simply save up some money. Now, there are four methods that we will be talking about today. The first would be about surveys.

Surveys

Now, this method has got to be one of the easiest ways someone can make money online. What you have to do to make money with this method is to have a PayPal account and some spare time. Now, most of the companies want people's opinions on things, to optimize their ad campaign or product so to do that they are willing to pay people money to survey them. Now the payout isn't a lot, but it is something you can use to make some side income online.

Some of the top websites I recommend you get into, if you want to make money with online surveys would be:

1. Vindale Research

2. Opinion Outpost

3. Swagbucks

Now, I have personally made $100 in a month with Vindale on the side, and it totally works so make sure you consider it, but regardless of which website you use out of the three, you will make money.

Please don't expect to make thousands of dollars a month on online surveys, yes they can make you money but not more than $300 a month even if you put in a lot of work, as there is a limit to how many surveys you can do in a day.

Amazon MTurk

Also known as Amazon Mechanical Turk, it is a transparent marketplace where you can go in as a worker and start earning some money. It isn't so hard and could yield you some good money, perhaps even more than using online surveys as your cash flow tool. What you do is quite simple you first make an account, and you start looking for jobs, the jobs are pretty simple like go like a post or retweet. They are jobs anyone can do, and they pay out anywhere from $0.10 to $100 per job.

There was an average done online for people working on MTurk, and they found out that people were making around $6 to 10 an hour after they became more seasoned. Which is great! Most people don't even earn that much on their real job. So make sure to utilize this if you want to make some money on the side, and just a heads up the account takes around two to three days to activate so make sure to factor in that time.

Transcription

If you're good at writing and you have the good sense of hearing then this might be the answer for you, transcriptions jobs are simply you listening to audio and typing down precisely what they say. The payout is quite good. You can expect to make around $2,000 a month with this job opportunity. It is easy money for anyone. If you have a computer, you can do it.

One of the websites I recommend you look into would be transcribed me, it is a great place to get your feet wet and start earning some money.

Fiverr

Fiver is honestly one of the best websites you can use—regardless of what you are looking for if you want to get a job done or if you are looking to earn money. Not only it is an easy way to earn money, but you have lots of options—so if there is anything you can think about that you are good at, then you most definitely can make money with the help of Fiverr.

For instance, if you think you are good at writing, you can post a job application on writing and set your price, and people will start purchasing your services. Now, if you're not good at anything—or at least from what you think—then you should do something like social proofing, wherein you will be providing people with social traffic. The best part of this particular job is that you don't even need to have a huge following—you can make some money even only having 100 to 200 followers. Yes, people pay for it.

Now, to give you a rough idea on how much you can make on Fiverr, it will depend on person to person and job to job—you can make anywhere from $100 a month to $10,000 a month. Thus, if this is something that will interest you, then do it!

The reason why I wrote this short chapter was to show you how easy it is to make money despite having small means. I know that some of the readers here merely want to earn some cash quickly but don't have any money to invest in any of the significant businesses mentioned in the earlier chapters—hence the reason why I came up with this chapter. With that being said, I want you to remember that money can be made anywhere and anytime—all you need is the willpower and determination to do it for yourself. I just gave you some fantastic ways to make money. No more can you make excuses saying you don't have the funds to start your own business or any of that. You now have every single tool in your power to make money to go out there and do it. It *is* possible—even for you!

Conclusion

Now, to conclude this amazing book, I would just like to remind you how easy it is to make money. People don't realize the fact that whatever they need to make, money is right in front of them. If you really want to, you can go online right now and start making money today—I just showed over ten ways on how to. However, remember that it takes some effort to get there.

Just like anything in life, the things you want aren't free. This doesn't just mean in terms of spending money—it could also mean putting in the time and effort to actually do it. Look, you can make money online easily—you just have to put in the time and the effort before you can start to *spontaneously* earn it. It won't be an easy way, but it will totally be worth it!

If we look at the top earners in the world, they all started from the bottom. They all worked their butts off to get to where they are right now. The truth is—yes, any business can become passive once you get the ball rolling— but in the beginning, it is all hard work. For example, building a company or building a brand takes time and effort, so make sure you are aware of what you are getting yourself into with any business you'll partake in.

Finally, I would like to say that in order to make things work in this book, you need to get yourself up of the bed or sofa and start working. These amazing ideas won't start working by themselves—you need to take massive actions *now* before it's too late. Wait no more and pick yourself up off the bed or wherever you are—pick an idea and start working on it day in and day out. Most importantly, don't *ever* give up—everything takes time to materialize.

Thanks again for everyone who bought this book. I really appreciate it, and I hope this book truly changed your life!